Quick Start Guides

The Es SUGAR FREE
SLOW COOKER
Recipe Book

A Quick Start Guide To Healthy Sugar Free Slow Cooking.

90 Simple And Delicious Calorie Counted Recipes For Weight Loss and Good Health.

First published in 2017 by Erin Rose Publishing

Text and illustration copyright © 2017 Erin Rose Publishing

Design: Julie Anson

ISBN: 978-1-911492-10-8

A CIP record for this book is available from the British Library.

DISCLAIMER: This book is for informational purposes only and not intended as a substitute for the medical advice, diagnosis or treatment of a physician or qualified healthcare provider. The reader should consult a physician before undertaking a new health care regime and in all matters relating to his/her health, and particularly with respect to any symptoms that may require diagnosis or medical attention.

While every care has been taken in compiling the recipes for this book we cannot accept responsibility for any problems which arise as a result of preparing one of the recipes. The author and publisher disclaim responsibility for any adverse effects that may arise from the use or application of the recipes in this book. Some of the recipes in this book include nuts and eggs. If you have an egg or nut allergy it's important to avoid these. It is recommended that children, pregnant women, the elderly or anyone who has an immune system disorder avoid eating raw eggs.

CONTENTS

Recipes

SWEETS, DESSERTS & SNACKS

INTRODUCTION

If you are one of the many people worldwide, who have cut out sugar from your diet and are looking to expand your range of recipes, you can do so with this sugar-free slow cooker recipe book. If, however, you are new to a sugar-free diet and you are daunted at where to start – welcome! This **Quick Start Guide** is a great place to find sugar-free slow cooker breakfasts, light bites, main meals and desserts which are simple, healthy and very very tasty!

Our aim is to provide you with all the information you need to make sugar-free eating easy, so if you think you don't have the time to prepare tasty dishes, think again. Combining sugar-free cooking with slow cooking is a great way to ensure you have something guilt-free to eat in no time at all. Delicious slow-cooked meals can be cooking while you get on with life and can be waiting for you when you get home allowing you the time to relax and enjoy the delicious dish you've prepared with little effort.

Sugar-free eating has become a way of life for some many people and it's not a diet per se, it's a lifestyle choice that many have adopted. There's so much evidence that sugar is bad for you, more than we previously knew and a recent headline 'Is Sugar A Food Or A Drug?' sums up how addictive the white stuff's effects on the body can be. So, if you've joked that you're a sugar addict you might be more right than you know. The good news is you can kick sugar for good, balance your mood and energy levels and gain a new lease of life!

Why Go On A Sugar-Free Diet?

Almost every day there is more and more evidence and media coverage that sugar consumption is linked with obesity in adults and children, heart disease, increased abdominal fat, cancer, type 2 diabetes, stress, anxiety and mental health issues including Alzheimer's disease.

There are two main reasons why we consume too much sugar, one is that it is added to a huge number of foods we regularly buy in the supermarket, often unaware of its hidden sugar and two is that it's as addictive. Sugar produces reactions in the brain which creates dependency and over time the body becomes desensitised and needs even more to be satisfied. The body is unable to metabolise large quantities of sugar and causes degenerative diseases due to the build-up of acid. Reducing sugar intake can benefit other health issues too such as acne, insomnia, fatigue, mood swings and Polycystic Ovaries Syndrome.

So, it's time to kick the sugar habit and remove the empty calories from your diet. You can reduce or cut out sugar from your diet in a way which suits you. Most people find it easier to cut it out completely as even eating small quantities can trigger cravings and imbalance in blood sugar which make it difficult to stick to. Going cold turkey and quitting sugar completely may be the easiest way for you.

You may be thinking there are so many sugar-free products on the supermarket shelves this has got to be easy! Don't be fooled. 'Sugar-free' products often are laden with other products which may be sugar under another name or sweetened with artificial sweeteners which have been linked with chronic health problems. Truly, the best way to go sugar-free is to home-cook so that you know what you are eating is really good for you because you added the healthy ingredients yourself.

What Can't I Eat?

So, if you are ready to make a change for the better you can get started straight away and take a step towards better health. First of all, you need to know what you can and can't eat so we've provided a comprehensive list, to make life simpler.

FOODS TO AVOID

- Any food containing sugar.

- Avoid all fizzy and sugary drinks, including diet drinks with artificial sweeteners such as, aspartame, xylitol, sucralose, cyclamates, saccharin, acesulfame potassium.

- Avoid dried fruit, including apricots, dates, raisins, sultanas, apples, bananas, mango, pineapple, figs etc.

- Pure or concentrated fruit juices.

- Cakes, biscuits, muesli, granola, muffins, chocolate bars, sweets, cereal bars and breakfast cereals (where sugar is added to the ingredients).

- Honey, syrup, jams and preserves.

- Ready-made sauces like relish, ketchup, sweet chilli sauce, marinades and barbecue sauce.

- Avoid ripe tropical fruit such as mango and papaya.

- Steer clear of beer, wine, spirits, liqueurs, cordials, milk shakes, fizzy drinks and hot chocolates.

What Can I Eat?

BELOW IS A LIST OF FOODS YOU CAN EAT.

- All meats including beef, chicken, lamb, pork and turkey. Avoid breaded and battered meat products.

- Fresh fish such as tuna, haddock, cod, anchovies, salmon, trout, sardines, herring and sole. Shellfish such as prawns, mussels and crab. Avoid breaded or battered fish products.

- Eggs

- Tofu

- Nuts inc. peanut butter, cashew butter and almond butter

- Seeds

Fats
- Butter

- Coconut Oil

- Olive Oil

- Ghee

- Full-fat dairy produce; cheeses, Greek yogurt, sour cream, clotted cream, mascarpone, crème fraîche, double cream (heavy cream) single cream.

Fruit – Maximum 2 pieces of low sugar fruit per day
- Apples

- Apricots

- Bananas

- Blackberries

- Blackcurrants

- Blueberries

- Cherries

- Grapefruit

- Kiwi

- Kumquat

- Lemons

- Limes

- Melon

- Oranges

- Peaches

- Pears

- Plums

- Pomegranate

- Raspberries

- Redcurrants

- Strawberries

Vegetables

- Avocados

- Asparagus

- Aubergine (Eggplant)

- Bean Sprouts

- Broccoli

- Broad Beans

- Brussels Sprouts

- Cabbage

- Cauliflower

- Celery

- Courgette (Zucchini)

- Cucumber

- Kale

- Leeks

- Lettuce

- Mushrooms

- Pak Choi (Bok Choy)

- Peppers (Bell Peppers)

- Radish

- Root veg; such as parsnips, beetroots and carrots, in moderation as they have a higher carbohydrate content.

- Runner Beans

- Spinach

- Spring Onions (Scallions)

- Olives

- Onions

- Rocket (Arugula)

- Watercress

Drinks

- Tea

- Coffee

- Coconut Water

- Fruit Teas

- Green Tea

- Water

- Almond Milk

- Rice Milk

- Soya Milk

Dressings & Condiments

- Fresh herbs and spices

How To Read The Labels

We have provided you with a list of sugar alias names so you can weed out the hidden sugars in products during your weekly shop. This is really important and quite an eye-opener if you are new to tracking down stealth sugars in everyday foods.

> If you need any proof that you may be consuming more sugar than you thought, try this little experiment. Tot up how much sugar you eat on an average day and don't limit it to spoonfuls of sugar in hot drinks or cereals, read the labels of everything you eat, including ready-meals to smoothies and fruit juices.
>
> **Your daily sugar intake is between 24g-36g a day, which equates to 6-9 teaspoons of sugar.**

You can identify sugar on product labels under the following names:

- Agave nectar or agave syrup
- Invert sugar syrup
- Brown sugar
- Cane sugar
- Cane juice crystals
- Dextrin
- Dextrose
- Glucose
- Glucose syrup
- Sucrose
- Fructose
- Fructose syrup
- Maltodextrin
- Barley malt
- Beet sugar
- Corn syrup
- High Fructose Corn Syrup
- Caramel
- Date sugar
- Palm sugar
- Malt syrup
- Refiners syrup
- Fruit juice concentrate
- Carob syrup
- Golden syrup
- Refiners syrup
- Ethylmaltol
- Maple syrup
- Treacle
- Molasses

Making The Most Of Your Slow Cooker

Many slow cookers sit idle at home, forgotten about and hibernating in a kitchen cupboard but with a little inspiration and only a few minutes preparation time, you can get so much more out of your slow cooker. The capability of slow cookers isn't limited to traditional casseroles. You can make frittatas, rice dishes, baked potatoes, pies and desserts.

One of the benefits of slow cooking is that it allows the flavours to infuse slowly, maximising flavour and increasing tenderness. Although slow cooking is ideal if you are catering for a family you can easily double the quantities if you are cooking for larger groups. But let's not forget about the solo chef who might be put off cooking bigger portions than they need – leftovers are a great way to fill your fridge or freezer with a quick and healthy warm-up meal. Simply freeze dishes into single portions using a container or freezer bags, ready to re-heat when you don't have much time.

Slow cookers, also known as crockpots, come in a variety of sizes. The important thing is to follow the guidelines specific to your model. For instance, many of them don't require pre-heating but check your manufacturer's instructions in case yours does and if it does, allow for this in the preparation time. Cooking time is generally lengthy and approximate and a short time either way won't really impact most dishes.

Some slow cookers have 4 settings ranging from warm to high and others less. Bear in mind that if you do wish to preheat your slow cooker, do so using the highest setting which will take less time, remembering you may wish to lower the setting during the cooking process. You can have the freedom to choose whether to set the cooker on low or high depending on your schedule, just take into account that meat, chicken and fish dishes need to be thoroughly cooked and longer cooking time will make meats, stews and casseroles more tender and juicy. If you are even in doubt as to whether something is completely cooked, test it using a skewer or kitchen thermometer.

Some slow cooker models do a timer which is handy so you can make sure dishes get the right cooking time, particularly if you are going to be at work or cooking overnight.

Cooking times are a guide only and will vary between different cookers. Always use some liquid in the slow cooker and you can use it as a ban marie if you are making breads and desserts. Try not to keep removing the lid of your cooker. If you remove the lid frequently bear in mind you may be losing a lot of moisture so you may need to add a little extra if it looks like it's drying. You might also need to increase cooking time. Many of our recipes do not require 'browning' in a pan before transferring it to the slow cooker but in some cases it can improve the look of the chicken or meat but it's really a personal choice. If an excessive amount of fat comes out of meat you can always skim it off towards the end of cooking.

We've used cornflour as a thickener in some of our recipes and you can use less or more depending on how you like the consistency of your gravies and sauces.

Stocking Up Your Cupboards

Preparing ahead of time and stocking your shelves with essential ingredients will make it easier for you to make a wide variety of dishes based on a few non-perishable ingredients. Here are a few easily stored items to help you pull together a tasty sugar-free slow cooked meal. First of all, it's best to go through your cupboards, checking the labels to eliminate all foods containing sugar, it will remove temptation and help you stay sugar-free.

Keep a plentiful supply of fresh produce including plenty of vegetables, eggs, cheese and meats. You can do this in the fridge or the freezer and while our recipes mostly include the use of fresh vegetables you can swap these for the frozen variety if you like. Also you can use chicken, fish and meat from the freezer too if you don't want to overstock your fridge.

Herbs & Spices

Cinnamon

Cumin

Oregano

Thyme

Chilli powder and chilli flakes

Nutmeg

Mixed herbs

Coriander (cilantro) ground and fresh

Paprika

Star anise

Chinese Five Spice

Ginger (ground and/or fresh root ginger)

Tinned Foods

Lentils

Cannellini beans

Kidney beans

Tinned chopped tomatoes (with no sugar added)

Coconut milk

Oils

Olive oil

Sesame oil

Condiments & Others

Cornflour

Plain flour (all-purpose flour)

Stevia sweetener

Worcestershire sauce

Tomato purée (paste)

Soy sauce

Mustard

Vanilla extract

Breakfast

Spiced Apple Porridge

Ingredients

100g (3½ oz) oats
25g (1oz) butter
2 apples, peeled, cored and chopped
2 teaspoons ground cinnamon
½ teaspoon ground nutmeg
½ teaspoon salt
600mls (1 pint) water
250mls (8fl oz) milk
Butter for greasing

SERVES 2

352 calories per serving

Method

Coat the inside of the slow cooker with the butter. Add all the ingredients to the slow cooker and stir well. Cook on low overnight for a delicious, warming porridge in the morning without any fuss. You can easily increase the quantities to make a larger batch and store it in the fridge, ready to use.

French Toast Breakfast Casserole

SERVES 4

372 calories per serving

Ingredients

50g (2oz) butter

8 slices of wholemeal bread

6 eggs

2 large bananas, peeled and mashed

1 teaspoon vanilla extract

1/4 teaspoon cinnamon

1/4 teaspoon nutmeg

360mls (12fl oz) double cream (or crème fraîche)

Butter for greasing

Method

Grease the bowl of a slow cooker with a little oil or butter. Spread each of the slices of bread with butter then cut them in to triangles. Lay the bread over the bottom of the slow cooker. In a bowl, combine the eggs, cream, vanilla, cinnamon and nutmeg. Pour the mixture over the bread and sprinkle with a little cinnamon and nutmeg. Cook on low for 4 hours or on high for 2 hours. As an alternative, try replacing the bananas with an apple or berries and have fun experimenting with your favourite.

Meaty Breakfast Casserole

Ingredients

100g (3½ oz) Cheddar cheese
100g (3½ oz) plain (unflavoured) yogurt
100g (3½ oz) ham (or bacon)
75g (3oz) spinach leaves
75g (3oz) mushrooms, chopped
8 eggs
8 good quality sausages, chopped
1 teaspoon dried mixed herbs
100mls (3½ fl oz) milk
Sea salt
Freshly ground black pepper
Butter for greasing

SERVES 6

280 calories per serving

Method

Grease and line the inside of the slow cooker bowl with grease-proof paper. In a large bowl, combine the eggs with the milk, yogurt and herbs. Add in the cheese, sausages, ham (or bacon), mushrooms and spinach. Season with salt and pepper. Pour the mixture into the bowl. Cook on low for 4-5 hours or on high for 2-3 hours.

Vegetarian Breakfast Casserole

Ingredients

675g (1 1/2 lb) potatoes, peeled and finely sliced

150g (5oz) Cheddar cheese, grated (shredded)

8 eggs

2 teaspoons mustard

1 clove of garlic, crushed

1 teaspoon pepper

1 teaspoon salt

1 teaspoon dried mixed herbs

1 teaspoon sweet paprika

1 onion, finely chopped

1 red pepper (bell pepper) deseeded and chopped

1 yellow pepper (bell pepper) deseeded and chopped

1 small head of broccoli, roughly chopped

600mls (1 pint) milk

Butter for greasing

SERVES 6

383 calories per serving

Method

Grease and line the inside bowl of a slow cooker with grease-proof paper. Line the potato slices over the bottom of the pot. Scatter a layer of peppers, onion, broccoli and cheese on top. Add another layer of sliced potatoes and scatter the remaining vegetables on top. In a bowl, mix together the eggs, mustard, garlic, pepper, paprika, salt, herbs and milk. Pour the egg mixture over the ingredients in the slow cooker. Cook on low for 4-5 hours.

Quinoa & Coconut Porridge

SERVES 2

240 calories per serving

Ingredients

150g (5oz) quinoa
1 teaspoon vanilla extract
1 teaspoon stevia sweetener (optional)
1/2 teaspoon cinnamon
400mls (14fl oz) water
200mls (7fl oz) coconut milk
Pinch of salt

Method

Place all of the ingredients into the bowl of a slow cooker and stir well. Cook on low for 8 hours. Enjoy. Makes a high protein alternative to oaty porridge and you can add toppings such as berries or chopped nuts.

Coconut, Almond & Raspberry Porridge

SERVES 2

374 calories per serving

Ingredients

250g (9 oz) fresh raspberries
100g (3½ oz) oats
2 tablespoons desiccated (shredded) coconut
1 tablespoon ground almonds (almond meal/almond flour)
1 teaspoon vanilla extract
½ teaspoon cinnamon
Pinch of salt
600mls (1 pint) water
250mls (8fl oz) milk

Method

Place the oats, coconut, almonds, cinnamon, salt, vanilla, water and milk to the bowl and mix well. Cook on low overnight. When ready to serve, scatter the raspberries into the porridge and save a few as garnish. Eat straight away.

Feta & Tomato Frittata

Ingredients

150g (5oz) mushrooms, sliced

125g (4oz) feta cheese, crumbled

100g (3½oz) cherry tomatoes (halved)

8 eggs

4 spring onions (scallions) chopped

2 tablespoons grated (shredded) Parmesan cheese

1 large handful of fresh spinach, finely chopped

1 tablespoon butter

½ teaspoon mixed herbs

¼ teaspoon salt

¼ teaspoon pepper

Butter for greasing

SERVES 4

245 calories per serving

Method

Coat the bowl of a slow cooker with butter. Whisk the eggs in a large bowl then stir in all the remaining ingredients. Pour the egg mixture into the slow cooker. Cook on high for 2 hours or on low for around 4 hours. Serve and enjoy.

Soups & Light Meals

Turkey & Vegetable Broth

Ingredients

450g (1lb) fresh turkey breast steaks, chopped

400g (14oz) tin of chopped tomatoes

200g (7oz) brown lentils, rinsed

100g (3½ oz) pearl barley

75g (3oz) cabbage, finely chopped

3 stalks of celery, finely chopped

2 cloves of garlic, chopped

1 carrot, peeled and diced

1 onion, peeled and chopped

1 handful of fresh spinach leaves

1 teaspoon dried mixed herbs

2 tablespoons tomato purée (paste)

1 small handful of fresh parsley, chopped

1200mls (2 pints) chicken stock (broth)

300mls (½ pint) hot water

Sea salt

Freshly ground black pepper

SERVES 6

208 calories per serving

Method

Place all of the ingredients, except the parsley, salt and pepper, into a slow cooker and stir well. Cook on high for around 6 hours. If you prefer your soup thinner you can add a little extra hot water. Sprinkle in the parsley and stir well. Season with salt and pepper. Serve into bowls.

Tomato & Red Pepper Soup

Ingredients

350g (12oz) tomatoes on the vine, stalk removed and chopped

2 red peppers (bell peppers), deseeded and chopped

2 onions, peeled and chopped

1 sweet potato, peeled and chopped

2 cloves of garlic, crushed

400mls (14fl oz) hot vegetable stock (broth)

Sea salt

Freshly ground black pepper

SERVES 4

105
calories
per serving

Method

Place all of the vegetables into a slow cooker and pour the hot vegetable stock (broth) on top. Cook on high for around 4 hours or cook on low for 6-7 hours. Season with salt and pepper. Using a hand blender, process the soup until until smooth. Serve and enjoy.

Lentil & Vegetable Soup

Ingredients

100g (3½ oz) red lentils

3 stalks of celery, chopped

3 cloves of garlic, crushed

1 carrot, peeled and roughly chopped

1 onion, peeled and roughly chopped

1 sweet potato, peeled and chopped

1 potato, peeled and chopped

1 leek, washed and chopped

1 bay leaf

1 litre (1 ½ pints) hot vegetable stock (broth)

2 teaspoons tomato purée (paste)

2 teaspoons fresh parsley, chopped

Sea salt

Freshly ground black pepper

SERVES 4

106 calories per serving

Method

Place all of the vegetables, lentils and the garlic into a slow cooker and pour in the vegetable stock (broth). Stir in the tomato purée (paste) and bay leaf. Cook on high for around 6 hours or on low for 8-9 hours. Sprinkle in the parsley and season with salt and pepper. Remove the bayleaf and serve.

French Onion Soup & Cheese Croutons

Ingredients

- 100g (3½ oz) Gruyère cheese, grated (shredded)
- 6 large onions, peeled and finely sliced
- 4 slices baguette
- 3 cloves garlic, crushed
- 2 tablespoons olive oil
- 2 tablespoons Worcester sauce
- 750mls (1 ½ pints) hot chicken stock (broth)
- Pinch salt
- Freshly ground black pepper

SERVES 4

295 calories per serving

Method

Place the oil, onions, garlic, Worcester sauce, stock (broth), salt and pepper into a slow cooker and stir the mixture really well. Cook on low for around 4 hours. When ready to serve, place the bread slices until a hot grill (broiler) and toast it on one side. Turn it over and sprinkle some cheese on top then return it to the grill until the cheese has melted. Serve the cheese crouton on top of the soup and eat straight away.

Spicy Chicken & Chickpea Soup

Ingredients

- 450g (1lb) chicken fillets, cut into chunks
- 400g (14oz) tinned chopped tomatoes
- 1 red pepper (bell pepper), de-seeded and chopped
- 1 onion, peeled and chopped
- 2 cloves of garlic, crushed
- 1 teaspoon paprika
- 1 teaspoon ground cumin
- 1 teaspoon Harissa paste
- 275g (10oz) tinned chickpeas, drained
- 750mls (1 ½ pints) chicken stock (broth)
- 2 tablespoons fresh coriander (cilantro) leaves, chopped

SERVES 4

308 calories per serving

Method

Place the chicken into a slow cooker and add in the vegetables. Pour in the stock (broth) and stir in the garlic, spices and Harissa paste. Cook the soup on low for 8 hours or on high for around 5 hours. Sprinkle in the fresh coriander and stir. Serve on its own or with a dollop of plain (unflavoured) yogurt.

Seafood Chowder

Ingredients

450g (1oz) cod fillets, roughly chopped
400g (14oz) tin of chopped tomatoes
275g (10oz) potatoes, peeled and diced
25g (1oz) butter, melted
3 tablespoons plain flour (all-purpose flour)
2 stalks of celery, finely chopped
2 teaspoons dried parsley
1 onion, peeled and chopped
1 carrot, peeled and finely diced
1 teaspoon salt
1 teaspoon white pepper
600mls (1 pint) fish or vegetable stock (broth)
50mls (2 fl oz) double cream (heavy cream)
Splash of tabasco sauce

**SERVES
4**

338
calories
per serving

Method

Place the fish, potatoes, onion, celery and carrot into a slow cooker. Sprinkle in the salt, pepper, parsley, tomatoes and a splash of tabasco sauce. Pour in the stock (broth) and stir all the ingredients well. Cook on low for 7 hours and on high for 3 hours. In a small bowl, mix together the butter, cream and flour until it becomes smooth then slowly add the mixture the chowder, stirring continuously. Cook for 40 minutes. Serve into bowls and enjoy.

Minestrone Soup

Ingredients

- 400g (14oz) tinned chopped tomatoes
- 275g (10oz) tinned kidney beans, drained
- 50g (2oz) spaghetti, broken up
- 50g (2oz) green beans, chopped
- 2 carrots, peeled and finely chopped
- 1 onion, peeled and chopped
- 1 red pepper (bell pepper), de-seeded and chopped
- 1 small handful of fresh basil, chopped
- 1 tablespoon tomato purée (paste)
- 2 teaspoons paprika
- 1/2 teaspoon cayenne pepper
- 600mls (1 pint) hot vegetable stock (broth)

SERVES 4

145 calories per serving

Method

Place all of the ingredients, except the spaghetti pieces and basil, into a slow cooker and stir well. Cook on high for around 4 hours or on low for 6-7 hours. Add in the spaghetti pieces and mix well. Cook for around 15 minutes or until the spaghetti has softened. Stir in the basil and serve into bowls. Enjoy.

Cream of Pumpkin Soup

Ingredients

900g (2lb) fresh pumpkin, peeled and de-seeded

2 teaspoons butter

1 onion, peeled and chopped

1/4 teaspoon nutmeg

1/4 teaspoon ground ginger

1/4 teaspoon cinnamon

600mls (1 pint) vegetable stock (broth)

150mls (5fl oz) double cream (or crème fraîche)

Sea salt

Freshly ground black pepper

SERVES 6

166 calories per serving

Method

Cut the pumpkin into chunks and place it in the slow cooker. Add in the butter, onion, nutmeg, ginger, cinnamon and stock (broth). Stir well. Cook on low for 5-6 hours or on high for 3-4 hours. Using a hand blender or food processor, blitz the soup until smooth. Stir in the cream and season with salt and pepper. Serve and enjoy.

Tomato & Quinoa Soup

Ingredients

- 400g (14oz) tinned tomatoes
- 400g (14oz) butterbeans
- 175g (6oz) quinoa, rinsed well
- 1 onion, peeled and chopped
- 1 bay leaf
- 1 small handful of fresh parsley, chopped
- 3 cloves garlic, crushed
- ½ teaspoon dried basil
- ½ teaspoon dried oregano
- ½ teaspoon dried thyme
- 750mls (1 ½ pints) vegetable stock (broth)
- Sea salt
- Freshly ground black pepper

SERVES 4

171 calories per serving

Method

Place the tomatoes, quinoa, onion, butterbeans, garlic and herbs into a slow cooker. Pour in the vegetable stock (broth) and stir well. Season with salt and pepper. Cook on low for 7 hours or on high for 3 hours. Sprinkle in the parsley and remove the bay leaf before serving.

Thai Curry Soup

Ingredients

450g (1lb) skinless chicken breasts, cut into strips
125g (4oz) frozen peas
2 tablespoons green curry paste
2 tablespoons fish sauce
1 tablespoon peanut butter
1 red pepper (bell pepper), deseeded and sliced
1 onion, finely chopped
2.5cm (1 inch) chunk of fresh ginger, peeled and finely chopped
1 small handful of coriander (cilantro)
400mls (14fl oz) coconut milk
600mls (1 pint) chicken stock (broth)
Juice of 1/2 lime

SERVES 4

418 calories per serving

Method

In a bowl, combine the coconut milk with the curry paste, fish sauce, stock (broth) and peanut butter. Pour the mixture into a slow cooker. Add the chicken, onion, pepper and ginger. Cook on high for around 3 hours. Add the peas to the slow cooker and mix well. Cook for around 1 hour. Stir in the coriander (cilantro) and lime juice just before serving.

Cheesy Vegetable Soup

Ingredients

- 300g (11oz) crème fraîche
- 175g (6oz) Cheddar cheese, grated (shredded)
- 25g (1oz) cream cheese (full fat)
- 1 medium head of broccoli
- 2 carrots, peeled and grated (shredded)
- 1 onion, finely chopped
- 2 cloves of garlic, chopped
- 1 teaspoon dried mixed herbs
- 450mls (15 fl oz) chicken stock (broth)
- Sea salt
- Freshly ground black pepper

SERVES 4

312 calories per serving

Method

Place the carrots, onion, broccoli, cream cheese, stock (broth), garlic and herbs into a slow cooker and mix well. Cook on low for around 4 hours or on high for 2-3 hours. Stir in the crème fraîche. Transfer half of the soup to a deep bowl and using a hand blender, process it until it is smooth. Return the mixture to the slow cooker and stir it in thoroughly. Warm the soup further if you need to. Season with salt and pepper. Serve it into bowls with a sprinkling of cheese on top. Enjoy.

Pea Soup

Ingredients

450g (1b) frozen peas
3 tablespoons crème fraîche
1 leek, washed and finely chopped
1 onion, peeled and finely chopped
1 stalk of celery, finely chopped
1 small handful of fresh mint leaves, chopped
750mls (1 ½ pints) vegetable stock (broth)
Sea salt
Freshly ground black pepper

SERVES
4

131
calories
per serving

Method

Place the onion, leek, celery and peas into a slow cooker and pour on the stock (broth). Cook on high for 3-4 hours or on low for 5-6 hours. Stir in the chopped mint and let it cook for 10 minutes. Season with salt and pepper. Using a hand blender, blitz the soup until smooth. Stir in the crème fraîche. Serve and eat straight away.

Creamy Celeriac Soup

Ingredients

- 2 onions, peeled and chopped
- 1 head of celeriac, peeled and finely chopped
- 1 potato, peeled and chopped
- 1 clove of garlic, chopped
- 1 teaspoon dried parsley
- 750mls (1 ½ pints) hot vegetable stock (broth)
- Sea salt
- Freshly ground black pepper
- 2 tablespoons crème fraîche

**SERVES
6**

113
calories
per serving

Method

Place all of the vegetables into a slow cooker and pour on the vegetable stock (broth) and add the garlic and dried parsley. Cook on low for 6 hours or on high for around 3 hours. Using a hand blender, process the soup until smooth. Season with salt and pepper then stir in the crème fraîche. Serve and eat immediately.

Spanish Chorizo & Peppers

Ingredients

500g (1lb 2oz) chorizo sausage, cut into slices

150g (5oz) tomato purée (paste)

6 cloves garlic, crushed

2 green peppers (bell peppers), seeded and chopped

2 red onions, peeled and chopped

600mls (1 pint) vegetable stock (broth)

1 teaspoon white wine vinegar

**SERVES
6**

433
calories
per serving

Method

Scatter the sausage into a slow cooker; add the peppers, garlic, onion, tomato purée, vinegar, stock (broth) and water. Stir it well. Cook on low for 7 hours. This can be served on its own as a side dish or with vegetables, rice or potatoes.

Slow Cooked Dahl

Ingredients

- 300g (11oz) yellow split peas
- 200g (7oz) fresh tomatoes, chopped
- 2.5cm (1 inch) chunk of fresh ginger, peeled and finely chopped
- 4 cloves of garlic, chopped
- 2 teaspoons ground cumin
- 2 teaspoons curry powder
- 1 teaspoon ground turmeric
- 1 onion, peeled and chopped
- 1 red chilli, finely sliced
- 1 small handful fresh coriander (cilantro) leaves
- 700mls (1½ pints) hot vegetable stock
- Sea salt and freshly ground black pepper

SERVES 4

140 calories per serving

Method

Place all of the ingredients except the coriander (cilantro) into a slow cooker and stir well. Cook on high for 4 hours. Season with salt and pepper. Stir in the coriander (cilantro). Serve the dahl on its own or with rice.

Sugar-Free Pasta Sauce

Ingredients

2 x 400g (14oz) tins of chopped tomatoes
6 medium tomatoes, preferably on the vine, chopped
2 medium courgettes (zucchinis), chopped
1 small carrot, peeled and chopped
1 onion, peeled and chopped
1 bay leaf
1 handful fresh parsley, chopped
4 garlic cloves, chopped
1/2 teaspoon pepper
1/2 teaspoon salt
2 teaspoons dried mixed herbs

SERVES 8

46 calories per serving

Method

Place all of the ingredients into a slow cooker and cook on high for 3 hours. Remove the bay leaf and discard it. Use a hand blender or food processor and blitz the sauce until smooth. It can be added to pasta and meat dishes or easily stored in the fridge or freezer until ready to use. You can also double the quantities to make a larger batch if you want to freeze and store some.

Cranberry & Orange Sauce

189
calories
per batch

Ingredients

400g (14oz) bag of fresh cranberries

1 cinnamon stick

Freshly squeezed juice of 3 large oranges

1-2 teaspoons stevia powder or liquid

Method

Place all of the ingredients into a slow cooker and cook on low for 5 hours then remove the lid and continue cooking for another hour. Remove the cinnamon stick. Store in an airtight jar until ready to use. The perfect accompaniment to roast turkey!

Chickpea & Vegetable Bake

Ingredients

1 x 400g (14oz) tin of chickpeas (garbanzo beans)
1 x 400g (14oz) tin of chopped tomatoes
4 cloves of garlic, chopped
2 large courgettes (zucchinis), thickly chopped
2 sweet potatoes, peeled and chopped
2 teaspoons ground coriander (cilantro)
1 onion, peeled and chopped
1 medium aubergine (eggplant), thickly chopped
1 red pepper (bell pepper), deseeded and chopped
1 green pepper (bell pepper), deseeded and chopped
1 bunch of fresh basil, chopped
Sea salt
Freshly ground black pepper

SERVES 4

252 calories per serving

Method

Place all of the ingredients, except for the fresh basil, salt and pepper, into a slow cooker and stir well. Cook on low for 6 hours. Season with salt and pepper. Sprinkle in the basil and mix well. Serve on its own or as a side dish.

Garlic, Tomato & Mushroom Spaghetti

Ingredients

400g (14oz) tin of chopped tomatoes
300g (11oz) spaghetti
225g (8oz) mushrooms, sliced
3 cloves of garlic, finely chopped
1 stalks of celery, finely chopped
1 bunch of fresh basil leaves, chopped
1 tablespoon olive oil

SERVES 4

164 calories per serving

Method

Place all of the ingredients, except the spaghetti and basil, into a slow cooker and stir well. Cook on low for 5-6 hours. When you are nearly ready to serve, cook the spaghetti according to the instructions. Transfer the spaghetti to the slow cooker and sprinkle in the fresh basil. Stir well before serving.

Vegetable Korma

Ingredients

75g (3oz) green beans
75g (3oz) frozen peas
3 cloves of garlic, chopped
1 small cauliflower, broken into florets
1 onion, peeled and chopped
2 medium carrots, peeled and chopped
250mls (8fl oz) coconut milk
3 teaspoons mild curry powder
½ teaspoon sea salt
½ teaspoon cayenne pepper

**SERVES
4**

175
calories
per serving

Method

In a bowl, mix the coconut milk with the curry powder and stir to combine them. Place this and the ingredients into a slow cooker and stir well. Cook on low for 5-6 hours. Serve with cauliflower rice or brown rice.

Slow Cooked
Baked Potatoes

Ingredients

6 large baking potatoes
2 teaspoons butter
Sea salt

**SERVES
6**

231
calories
per serving

Method

Rub a little butter into the skin of each potato then sprinkle it with salt. Wrap each of the potatoes in tin foil, making sure they are completely sealed. Cook on high for around 4 hours or on low for 8 hours. Remove the potatoes from the slow cooker and remove the foil – take care as the potatoes will be piping hot. Serve with toppings such as cheese and chilli or avocado and bacon.

Smoked Haddock
& Pea Purée

Ingredients

SERVES
4

195
calories
per serving

275g (10oz) frozen peas
4 smoked haddock fillets
2 tablespoon crème fraîche or double cream
(heavy cream)
1 tablespoon chopped fresh mint leaves
175mls (6fl oz) fish or vegetable stock (broth)
Sea salt
Freshly ground black pepper

Method

Scatter the peas into a slow cooker and pour in the stock (broth). Set the haddock fillets on top of the peas. Cook on high for 2 hours or until the fish is completely cooked, tender and flaky. Remove the fish from the slow cooker and set aside, keeping it warm. Add the crème fraîche or cream. Using a hand blender, or food processor, blitz the peas until they are puréed. Season with salt and pepper. Serve the purée onto plates and place the haddock fillets on top. Eat straight away.

Stuffed Peppers

Ingredients

400g (14oz) tinned cannellini beans, drained

100g (3½ oz) brown rice

3 cloves of garlic, chopped

2 red peppers (bell peppers), top removed and de-seeded

2 yellow peppers (bell peppers), top removed and de-seeded

1 onion, peeled and finely chopped

1 teaspoon paprika

A handful of fresh basil

600mls (1 pint) vegetable stock (broth)

Sea salt

Freshly ground black pepper

SERVES 4

202 calories per serving

Method

Place the beans, rice, garlic, onion, basil and paprika into a bowl and mix well. Season with salt and pepper. Scoop some of the mixture into each of the peppers and place the lid back onto the peppers. Pour the hot vegetable stock (broth) into a slow cooker. Gently lower the peppers into the stock, keeping them upright. If your slow cooker is large you can roll up some tin foil into balls and insert them alongside the peppers to keep them upright. Cook on low for around 5 hours or until the rice is soft. Serve and enjoy.

Vegetable & Cannellini Bean Rice

Ingredients

- 400g (14oz) tin of cannellini beans, drained
- 200g (7oz) basmati rice, rinsed
- 175g (6oz) butternut squash, peeled and chopped
- 6 spring onions (scallions), chopped
- 2 medium tomatoes, finely chopped
- 1 green pepper (bell pepper), deseeded and chopped
- 1 red chilli, deseeded and finely chopped
- 1 small handful of chopped basil
- 1/2 teaspoon ground allspice
- 1/2 teaspoon garlic powder
- 1/2 teaspoon salt
- 1/2 teaspoon pepper
- 750mls (1 1/4 pints) vegetable stock (broth)

SERVES 4

243 calories per serving

Method

Place the rice and vegetables into a slow cooker. Add in the allspice, garlic, chilli, salt and pepper and the stock (broth) and mix well. Cook on high for 1 ¾-2 hours. Sprinkle in the basil and stir. Serve into bowls and enjoy.

Tomato & Turkey Meatballs

Ingredients

FOR THE MEATBALLS:

- 450g (1lb) minced (ground) turkey
- 50g (2oz) whole wheat breadcrumbs
- 50g (2oz) Parmesan cheese, grated
- 1 egg
- 2 tablespoons fresh parsley, chopped
- 2 tablespoons fresh basil, chopped
- Sea salt
- Freshly ground black pepper

FOR THE TOMATO SAUCE:

- 2 x 400g (2x14oz) tinned chopped tomatoes
- 3 cloves of garlic, crushed
- 2 tablespoons chopped fresh parsley
- 1 tablespoon chopped fresh basil
- 1/2 teaspoon chilli flakes
- Freshly ground black pepper
- 1 teaspoon salt

SERVES 4

329 calories per serving

Method

In a large bowl, combine the turkey, breadcrumbs, Parmesan cheese, egg, parsley, basil, salt, and pepper. Shape the mixture into small balls. Pour all of the ingredients for the sauce into the slow cooker and mix well. Gently add the turkey balls to the tomato sauce and spoon some of the sauce over the top. Cook on low for 5 hours.

Satay Chicken

Ingredients

- 450g (1lb) chicken breast fillet, cut into strips
- 75g (3oz) smooth peanut butter
- 6 cloves garlic, finely chopped
- 2 red peppers (bell peppers), deseeded and sliced
- 2.5cm (1 inch) chunk of fresh ginger, peeled and finely chopped
- 1 teaspoon chilli flakes (or less if you don't like it spicy)
- 250mls (8fl oz) chicken stock (broth)
- 75mls (3fl oz) soy sauce
- Juice of ½ lime

SERVES 4

326 calories per serving

Method

Place all of the ingredients, except the lime, into a slow cooker and mix it really well. Cook for about 6 hours on high and or until the chicken is completely cooked and tender. Stir in the lime juice. Serve with a green salad or brown rice.

Ratatouille

Ingredients

225g (8oz) cherry tomatoes
3 medium sized courgettes (zucchinis)
3 cloves of garlic, chopped
1 onion, peeled and chopped
1 aubergine (eggplant) chopped
2 red peppers (bell peppers), de-seeded and chopped
1 teaspoon dried Herbs de Provence
175mls (6fl oz) vegetable stock (broth)
A handful of fresh basil, chopped
1-2 teaspoons cornflour
2 teaspoons olive oil

SERVES 4

111 calories per serving

Method

Heat the olive oil in a frying pan, add the chopped onion and cook for 5 minutes. Transfer the onions to a slow cooker. Add all the remaining ingredients to the slow cooker, apart from the cornflour and the basil. Cook on high for 3 hours. Mix the cornflour with a tablespoon of cold water and stir it into the ratatouille. Cook for another 30 minutes. Stir in the fresh basil before serving.

Baked Beans

Ingredients

2 x 400g (2 x 14oz) tins of cannellini beans, drained
2 x 400g (2 x 14oz) tins of chopped tomatoes
25g (1oz) butter
4 strips of pancetta, finely chopped
1 large onion, finely chopped
250mls (8fl oz) vegetable stock (broth)

SERVES 4

306 calories per serving

Method

Heat the butter in a frying pan, add the onion and pancetta and cook for a few minutes until the onion has softened. Transfer them to a slow cooker. Add the tomatoes, beans and vegetable stock (broth). Cook on low for 7 hours. Serve on their own or as a side dish. Makes a great sugar-free alternative to tinned baked beans.

Braised Savoy Cabbage & Peas

Ingredients

275g (10oz) frozen peas

1 head of savoy cabbage, finely chopped

1 large onion, peeled and chopped

200mls (7fl oz) vegetable stock (broth)

Sea salt

Freshly ground black pepper

SERVES 4

89
calories
per serving

Method

Place all of the ingredients into a slow cooker and stir well. Cook on high for 1-½ -2 hours. Season with salt and pepper, if required. Serve as a perfect accompaniment to meat, chicken and fish dishes.

Red Cabbage

Ingredients

2 apples, peeled cored and chopped

1 onion, peeled and chopped

1 head of red cabbage, finely chopped

1/2 teaspoon allspice

1/2 teaspoon cinnamon

120mls (4fl oz) red wine vinegar

Pinch of salt

SERVES 6

51 calories per serving

Method

Place all of the ingredients into the bowl of a slow cooker and give them a stir. Cook on low for 6-7 hours. Can be served warm or you can let it cool then spoon it into a lidded jar and store, ready to serve cold.

Casseroles, Risottos and Main Meals

Slow Cooked Spiced Ham

Ingredients

400g (14oz) cannellini beans, drained
1 gammon joint, approx. 450g (1lb) in weight
1 large onion, peeled and chopped
3 stalks of celery
3 sprigs of thyme
2 carrots, peeled and sliced
Zest of 1 orange
1 teaspoon dried parsley
1 teaspoon paprika
1/2 teaspoon chilli powder
1/2 teaspoon all-spice
450mls (15fl oz) vegetable stock (broth)
Sea salt
Freshly ground black pepper

SERVES 4

274 calories per serving

Method

Place the gammon in a slow cooker. Add the remaining ingredients, except the salt and pepper, and stir to mix them thoroughly. Cook on high for 6 hours. Season with salt and pepper. Shred the gammon using 2 forks to pull it apart. Serve with rice or new potatoes.

Beef Pot Roast

Ingredients

1 beef brisket joint, approximately 750g
in weight
2 onions, peeled and roughly chopped
2 carrots, peeled and roughly chopped
½ small swede, cut into chunks
1 tablespoon tomato purée (paste)
1-2 teaspoons cornflour
1 bay leaf
250mls (9fl oz) hot beef stock (broth)
Sea salt
Freshly ground black pepper

**SERVES
4**

477
calories
per serving

Method

In a small bowl, mix together the hot beef stock (broth) and the tomato purée (paste). Place the beef into the slow cooker and add the vegetables and bay leaf. Pour the stock (broth) mixture over the top. Cook the meat on low for 5-6 hours or until it is tender. Pour the meat juices into a small saucepan. Mix the cornflour in a cup with a spoonful or 2 or cold water then stir it into the meat juices to thicken the gravy. If you prefer your gravy thicker add a little extra cornflour paste. Remove the bay leaf before serving. Serve with roast or mashed potatoes and a heap of fresh vegetables.

Chicken & Butternut Squash

SERVES 4

262 calories per serving

Ingredients

- 175g (6oz) butternut squash, chopped
- 4 chicken breasts
- 2 cloves of garlic, crushed
- 2 x 400g (2 x 14oz) tins chopped tomatoes
- 1 teaspoon ground cumin
- 1 teaspoon ground cinnamon
- 1 large onion, peeled and chopped
- 1 teaspoon ground ginger
- 1/2 teaspoon sea salt
- 1/4 teaspoon ground black pepper
- 1 tablespoon olive oil

Method

In a large bowl combine the ginger, cumin, cinnamon, salt and pepper. Coat the chicken in the mixture. Heat the oil in a saucepan and add the chicken and brown it on all sides for a few minutes. Place the chicken into a slow cooker and add in the garlic, tomatoes, onion and butternut squash. Cook on low for 7 hours or on high for 4 hours.

Thai Salmon Curry

Ingredients

- 4 skinless salmon fillets
- 2.5cm (1 inch) chunk of ginger
- 1 onion, peeled and chopped
- 1 stalk of lemongrass, outer leaves removed
- 1 small handful of coriander (cilantro) leaves
- 1 tablespoon thai green curry paste
- 250mls (8fl oz) coconut milk
- 200mls (7fl oz) fish or vegetable stock (broth)
- Juice of 1 lime

SERVES 4

383 calories per serving

Method

Place the ginger, coriander (cilantro), lime juice, lemongrass, curry paste, coconut milk and onion into a food processor and blitz to a smooth paste. Place the salmon fillets into a slow cooker. Pour the curry mixture over the salmon. Cook on low for 2 ½ to 3 hours. The fish should be completely cooked and flake apart. Serve with rice and a sprinkling of coriander (cilantro).

Citrus Spiced Pork Fillet

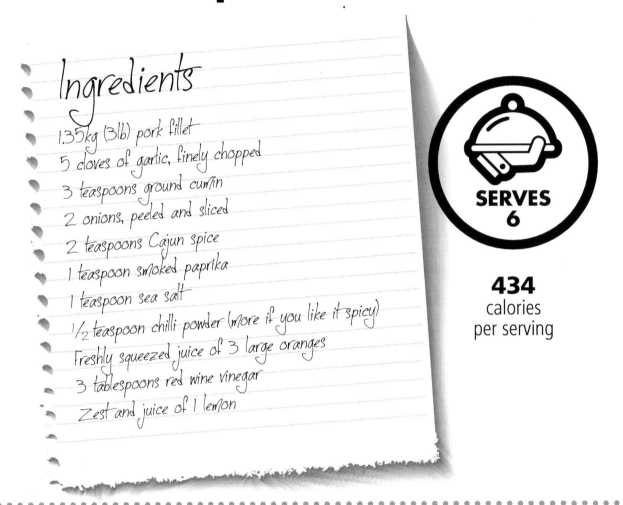

Ingredients

- 1.35kg (3lb) pork fillet
- 5 cloves of garlic, finely chopped
- 3 teaspoons ground cumin
- 2 onions, peeled and sliced
- 2 teaspoons Cajun spice
- 1 teaspoon smoked paprika
- 1 teaspoon sea salt
- 1/2 teaspoon chilli powder (more if you like it spicy)
- Freshly squeezed juice of 3 large oranges
- 3 tablespoons red wine vinegar
- Zest and juice of 1 lemon

**SERVES
6**

434
calories
per serving

Method

Place the garlic, cumin, Cajun spice, salt and paprika on a large plate and coat the pork in the mixture. Transfer the pork to a slow cooker. Pour in the vinegar, orange juice, lemon juice and zest. Scatter the onion on top. Cook on low for 7 hours. Serve and enjoy.

Sweet & Sour Chicken

Ingredients

- 450g (1lb) chicken breasts, cut into chunks
- 400g (14oz) tin of pineapple in natural juice (not syrup)
- 8 spring onions, (scallions), chopped
- 2 tablespoons tomato purée (paste)
- 2 tablespoons cornflour
- 1 red pepper (bell pepper), deseeded and chopped
- 1 yellow pepper (bell pepper), deseeded and chopped
- 4 tablespoons white wine vinegar
- 2 tablespoons olive oil
- 2 teaspoons soy sauce

SERVES 4

346
calories
per serving

Method

Drain the juice of the pineapple chunks and add the pineapple to a slow cooker and set aside the juice. Place the chicken, spring onions (scallions) and peppers into the slow cooker. In a small bowl, mix together the cornflour with 8 tablespoons of the natural pineapple juice you set aside together with the soy sauce, oil, vinegar and tomato purée (paste). Pour the mixture into the slow cooker. Cook on high for 5 hours. Serve with brown rice.

Prawn & Lemon Risotto

Ingredients

- 450g (1lb) prawns (shrimps), peeled and deveined
- 300g (11oz) risotto rice
- 200g (7oz) frozen peas, defrosted
- 25g (1oz) butter
- 1 medium onion, peeled and finely chopped
- 1/4 teaspoon chilli flakes
- Zest and juice 1 lemon
- 750mls (1 1/2 pints) hot fish or vegetable stock (broth)
- Sea salt
- Freshly ground black pepper

SERVES 4

327 calories per serving

Method

Grease the inside of a slow cooker with butter. Place the rice, prawns (shrimps), onion, peas, chilli and lemon into the slow cooker and mix well. Pour in the hot stock (broth) and stir. Cook on low for 5-6 hours or when the rice is creamy and the prawns are pink throughout. Season with salt and pepper. Serve and enjoy.

Chestnut Mushroom & Red Pepper Risotto

Ingredients

- 450g (1lb) chestnut mushrooms, sliced
- 300g (11oz) risotto rice
- 50g (2oz) Parmesan cheese, grated
- 25g (1oz) butter
- 1 onion, chopped
- 1 red pepper (bell pepper), chopped
- 600mls (1 pint) hot vegetable stock
- 1 small handful of fresh basil leaves, chopped

SERVES 4

284 calories per serving

Method

Grease the inside of a slow cooker with butter. Place the rice, onion, mushrooms and red pepper (bell pepper) into the slow cooker and pour in the hot stock (broth). Cook on low for 4-5 hours or until the rice is creamy and soft. Stir in the parmesan cheese and basil leaves before serving.

Lemon Chicken

Ingredients

4 skinless chicken breasts

4 potatoes, peeled and chopped

3 carrots, peeled and chopped

3 cloves of garlic, crushed

1 onion, peeled and chopped

1 teaspoon of mixed herbs

25g (1oz) butter

500mls (15fl oz) chicken stock (broth)

Juice of 1 lemon

Sea salt

Pepper

SERVES 4

387 calories per serving

Method

In a bowl, coat the chicken with the mixed herbs and season with salt and pepper. Heat the butter in a frying pan, add the chicken and quickly brown it slightly on either side. Place the chicken and all of the remaining ingredients into the slow cooker. Cook on high for 5-7 hours.

Chinese Beef & Broccoli

Ingredients

450g (1lb) beef steak, cut into strips
3 cloves of garlic, chopped
1 medium head of broccoli, broken into florets
2 tablespoons cornflour
1/4 teaspoon chilli flakes
360mls (12 fl oz) beef stock (broth)
100mls (3 1/2 fl oz) soy sauce
1 tablespoon sesame oil
1/2 teaspoon ground ginger
2 star anise
Sea salt
Freshly ground black pepper

SERVES 4

335 calories per serving

Method

Place the beef, soy sauce, stock (broth), chilli, garlic, oil, star anise and ginger into a slow cooker and stir well to mix all the ingredients. Cook on low for around 4 hours. Mix the cornflour with 2-3 tablespoons of cold water and mix to a smooth paste. Stir the cornflour paste into the beef mixture. Cook for another 20 minutes or until the sauce has thickened. In the meantime, place the broccoli into a steamer and cook for 5 minutes. Add the broccoli to the mixture. Season with salt and pepper and serve.

Creamy Quinoa & Tomato Chicken

Ingredients

- 450g (1lb) chicken breast, diced
- 175g (7oz) quinoa
- 100g (3½ oz) cream cheese
- 6 medium tomatoes, chopped
- 2 red peppers (bell peppers), deseeded and chopped
- 1 onion, peeled and chopped
- 1 small handful of fresh basil leaves, chopped
- 400mls (14fl oz) chicken or vegetable stock (broth)
- Sea salt
- Freshly ground black pepper

SERVES 4

337 calories per serving

Method

Place all of the ingredients, except the basil, salt and pepper into a slow cooker and mix well. Season with salt and pepper. Cook on low for 6-7 hours. Sprinkle the basil into the pot and give it a stir. Serve with a little basil on top.

Jambalaya

Ingredients

450g (1lb) chicken breast fillets, roughly chopped

450g (1lb) cooked peeled prawns (shrimps)

350g (12oz) smoked pork sausage, chopped

2 x 400g (2 x 14oz) tins chopped tomatoes

6 stalks of celery, finely chopped

2 teaspoons dried oregano

2 teaspoons dried parsley

2 teaspoons Cajun seasoning

1 onion, chopped

1 green pepper (bell pepper), chopped

1 teaspoon cayenne pepper

250mls (8fl oz) chicken stock (broth)

SERVES
6

394
calories
per serving

Method

Place all of the ingredients into a slow cooker and mix well. Cook on low for around 8 hours or on high for 5-6 hours. Serve with brown rice.

Lamb Shanks

Ingredients

50g (2oz) plain flour (all-purpose flour)
4 lamb shanks
4 fresh sprigs rosemary
3 large carrots, peeled and roughly chopped
2 onions, peeled and chopped
2 fresh bay leaves
1 tablespoon Worcestershire sauce
1 tablespoon tomato purée (paste)
1 clove of garlic, chopped
600mls (1 pint) beef or vegetable stock (broth)
2 tablespoons olive oil
Sea salt
Freshly ground black pepper

SERVES 4

359 calories per serving

Method

Place the flour into a bowl and coat the lamb shanks in it. Season with salt and pepper. Heat the oil in a frying pan and cook the lamb shanks on high for around 4 minutes to brown them. Place the lamb and the juices from the pan into a slow cooker. Add the remaining ingredients to the slow cooker. If necessary, add more hot water to make sure the lamb shanks are covered. Cook on low for 7-8 hours when the lamb is cooked and tender.

Tender 'Roast' Chicken

Ingredients

1 large chicken
1 large onion, peeled and sliced
1 teaspoon paprika
Sea salt
Freshly ground black pepper

SERVES 4

396
calories
per serving

Method

Scatter the onion slices in the slow cooker and add the chicken. Sprinkle the chicken with the paprika and season it with salt and pepper. Cook on low for 6-8 hours on low. The chicken should be tender and falling off the bone. So simple and so delicious!

Sausage & Lentil Casserole

Ingredients

450g dried lentils

400g (14oz) tin chopped tomatoes, drained

1.1kg (2½ lb) good quality sausages,
cut into thick chunks

1 carrot, chopped

2 stalks of celery, chopped

1 litre (1 ½ pints) hot beef stock (broth)

600mls (1 pint) hot water

**SERVES
6**

607
calories
per serving

Method

Place all of the ingredients into a slow cooker and stir it well. Cook on low for 6-8 hours or on high for 4-5 hours. Serve on its own or with mashed potatoes.

Pork, Apple & Ginger Chops

Ingredients

6 boneless pork chops

3 apples, peeled, cored and sliced

2 onions, peeled and finely chopped

1 teaspoon ground ginger

120mls (4fl oz) soy sauce

3 tablespoons tomato purée (paste)

2 cloves of garlic, chopped

Sea salt

Pepper

**SERVES
6**

213
calories
per serving

Method

Place the chops on the bottom of a slow cooker. Place the soy sauce and tomato purée (paste) into a small bowl, mix it well then pour it over the pork. Scatter the onions, apples, ginger and garlic into the slow cooker. Cook on a low setting for around 6 hours. Season with salt and pepper. Serve and enjoy.

Tandoori Chicken

Ingredients

6 skinless chicken breasts
1 tablespoon tandoori masala powder
1 tablespoon plain (unflavoured) yogurt
2 tablespoons lime juice
1 teaspoon olive oil
Sea salt

**SERVES
6**

183
calories
per serving

Method

Place the tandoori powder, yogurt, lime and salt into a bowl and stir well. Add the chicken breasts and coat them thoroughly in the mixture. Cover them and allow them to marinade in the fridge for at least 2 hours. Coat a slow cooker in the olive oil. Transfer the chicken to the slow cooker and cook on low for 6 hours. Serve with rice and salad.

Paella

Ingredients

400g (14oz) tin of chopped tomatoes
450g (1lb) frozen seafood mix, defrosted
300g (11oz) risotto rice, rinsed
2 cloves of garlic, chopped
1 small handful of fresh parsley, chopped
1 onion, peeled and chopped
1 teaspoon paprika
1 teaspoon smoked paprika
1/2 teaspoon dried oregano
1/2 teaspoon dried thyme
2 tablespoon lemon juice
1 tablespoon olive oil
900mls (1 1/2 pints) chicken or vegetable stock (broth)

SERVES 4

310
calories
per serving

Method

Heat the olive oil in a frying pan, add the onion and garlic and cook for 4 minutes. Add in the rice, paprika, oregano and thyme and stir to coat the rice in the mixture. Transfer the ingredients to a slow cooker. Add in the stock (broth) and tomatoes. Cook on high for 2 ½ hours. Add in the defrosted seafood and cook for at least 40 minutes or until the fish is completely cooked through. Add in the parsley and lemon juice just before serving.

Chicken 'Fried' Rice

Ingredients

- 350g (12oz) basmati rice
- 100g (3½ oz) frozen peas
- 25g (1oz) butter
- 6 spring onions (scallions), chopped
- 4 chicken breasts, chopped
- 3 cloves of garlic, finely chopped
- 2 carrots, peeled and finely diced
- ½ teaspoon paprika
- ¼ teaspoon sea salt
- ¼ teaspoon pepper
- 2 tablespoons soy sauce
- 450mls (15fl oz) vegetable stock (broth)

SERVES 4

419 calories per serving

Method

Heat the butter in a frying pan, add the chicken and cook it for 5 minutes, stirring constantly. Transfer the chicken to a slow cooker. Add all the ingredients on top of the chicken. Cook on high for 3 hours or until the chicken is completely cooked and the rice is tender. If you need to, add a little extra stock if it requires longer cooking time. Check the seasoning before serving.

Bolognese

Ingredients

450g (1lb) minced (ground) beef
450g (1lb) passata
175g (6oz) small mushrooms, halved
3 cloves of garlic, chopped
2 courgettes (zucchinis), finely diced
1 carrot, peeled and finely diced
1 onion, peeled and chopped
1 teaspoon dried basil
1 teaspoon dried oregano
175mls (6fl oz) beef stock (broth)
2 teaspoons olive oil
1 small handful of fresh basil
Sea salt
Freshly ground black pepper

SERVES 4

320
calories
per serving

Method

Heat the oil in a frying pan, add the onion and beef and brown it for 5 minutes. This step is optional as you can add the beef and onion directly to the slow cooker if you prefer. Transfer the beef and onion to a slow cooker and add all of the remaining ingredients, apart from the fresh basil. Cook on low for 8-9 hours. Stir in the fresh basil. Serve with whole-wheat or courgette (zucchini) spaghetti or roast vegetables. Enjoy.

Aromatic Pork Ribs

Ingredients

2 racks of pork ribs

2 onions, peeled and sliced

4 cloves of garlic, chopped

4 star anise

2 teaspoons ground ginger

150mls (5fl oz) hot water

2 tablespoons soy sauce

Sea salt

Pepper

**SERVES
4**

239
calories
per serving

Method

Place the ribs into a slow cooker and add the garlic, onions, ginger, soy sauce and star anise. Season with salt and pepper. Pour in the hot water and cook on low for 6-8 hours. Serve with dips or vegetables.

Chicken Tagine

Ingredients

450g (1lb) chicken breasts, chopped

400g (14oz) chickpeas (garbanzo beans), drained

3 cloves of garlic, chopped

2 large carrots, peeled and chopped

1 large sweet potato (peeled and diced)

1 onion, peeled and chopped

2.5cm (1 inch) chunk of fresh ginger, peeled and chopped

1 teaspoon ground cinnamon

1 teaspoon ground turmeric

1 teaspoon ground coriander

1 teaspoon ground cumin

600mls (1 pint) chicken stock (broth)

2 teaspoons olive oil (optional)

Sea salt

Freshly ground black pepper

SERVES 4

435 calories per serving

Method

Heat the olive oil in a frying pan, add the chicken and onion and brown it for a few minutes. This step is optional as you can add the chicken and onion straight to the slow cooker – whichever you prefer. Place all of the ingredients into a slow cooker and stir well. Season with salt and pepper. Cook on high for around 6 hours or until the chicken is tender. Serve with quinoa or couscous.

Beef & Barley Stew

Ingredients

SERVES 4

432 calories per serving

- 500g (1lb 2oz) stewing steak, diced
- 100g (3½ oz) barley
- 1 onion, peeled and chopped
- 3 carrots, peeled and chopped
- 3 parsnips, peeled and chopped
- 1 litre (1 ½ pints) hot beef stock (broth)
- 2 tablespoons Worcestershire sauce
- 1 tablespoon tomato purée (paste)
- 2 teaspoons olive oil (optional)
- Sea salt
- Freshly ground black pepper

Method

Heat the oil in a frying pan, add the meat and onion and brown it for 5 minutes – this is optional, however as they can be added straight to the slow cooker if you'd prefer. Place the meat, barley and vegetables into the slow cooker. Pour in the stock (broth) and stir in the tomato purée and Worcestershire sauce. Season with salt and pepper. Cook on low for 8-9 hours or until the beef is really tender.

Quinoa & Chicken Chilli

Ingredients

2 x 400g (2 x 14oz) tins of chopped tomatoes
400g (14oz) kidney beans, drained
450g (1lb) chicken breasts, chopped
125g (4oz) quinoa
3 cloves of garlic, chopped
1 large red pepper (bell pepper), chopped
1 onion, peeled and chopped
1 teaspoon ground cumin
1 teaspoon chilli powder
1 teaspoon Cajun seasoning
600mls (1 pint) chicken stock (broth)
Sea salt
Freshly ground black pepper

**SERVES
4**

448
calories
per serving

Method

Place all of the ingredients into a slow cooker and season with salt and pepper. Cook on low for 6-7 hours. Can be served with a dollop of guacamole, sour cream and a scattering of grated cheese.

Chicken Fajitas

Ingredients

- 400g (14oz) tin of chopped tomatoes
- 200g (7oz) Cheddar cheese, grated (shredded)
- 8 flour tortillas
- 5 cloves of garlic chopped
- 4 skinless chicken breasts, cut into strips
- 1 onion, peeled and chopped
- 1 red pepper (bell pepper) deseeded and chopped
- 1 green pepper (bell pepper) deseeded and chopped
- 1 yellow pepper (bell pepper) deseeded and chopped
- 2 teaspoons mild chilli powder
- 2 teaspoons ground cumin
- 2 teaspoons paprika
- 1 small handful of coriander (cilantro) chopped
- 1/2 teaspoon sea salt
- Juice of 1/2 lime

SERVES 4

466 calories per serving

Method

Spread the chopped tomatoes into a slow cooker. Stir in the onion, garlic, chilli powder, cumin, paprika and salt. Add the chicken breasts and coat them in the mixture. Scatter the chopped peppers over the top. Cook on high for around 4 hours, or until the chicken is tender and completely cooked. Stir in the coriander (cilantro) and lime juice. Serve into the tortillas with a sprinkling of cheese and you can add dollop of guacamole and sour cream too.

Lamb Hotpot

Ingredients

450g (1lb) potatoes, peeled and evenly sliced
450g (1lb) lean lamb steaks, cut into chunks
1 onion, peeled and chopped
1/2 medium sized, swede, peeled and finely diced
3 carrots, peeled and finely diced
175g (6oz) mushrooms, sliced
2 teaspoons cornflour
400mls (14fl oz) beef stock (broth)
2 tablespoons Worcestershire sauce
2 teaspoons olive oil (optional)
Sea salt
Freshly ground black pepper

**SERVES
4**

401
calories
per serving

Method

Heat the oil in a frying pan, add the meat and onion and brown it for 5 minutes. This step is optional as the lamb and onion can be added directly to the slow cooker. Transfer the lamb and onion to a slow cooker. Add the swede, carrots, mushrooms, Worcestershire sauce, stock (broth), salt and pepper. Mix together the cornflour with a tablespoon of water and stir it into the lamb mixture. Lay the potato slices in a circular pattern, with each slice just overlapping until the meat mixture is covered and all the potatoes have been used up. Cook on high for around 8 hours. You can add a knob of butter to the potatoes during cooking to keep them moist and golden if necessary.

Slow Cooked Autumn Vegetables

Ingredients

- 150g (5oz) cherry tomatoes, halved
- 150g (5oz) button mushrooms
- 125g (4oz) soya beans
- 125g (2oz) peas
- 3 cloves of garlic, peeled and chopped
- 2 carrots, peeled and roughly
- 1 whole beetroot, washed and roughly chopped
- 1 butternut squash, peeled and cut into chunks
- 1 medium broccoli, broken into florets
- 1 teaspoon dried thyme
- 1 teaspoon dried oregano
- 1 tablespoon olive oil
- Sea salt
- Freshly ground black pepper

SERVES 4

192 calories per serving

Method

Place all of the ingredients, except the tomatoes, into a slow cooker and mix them well. Cook on low for 3 hours. Add the tomatoes to the slow cooker and continue cooking for 30 minutes. Serve on its own or as an accompaniment to meat, chicken and fish dishes

Coconut & Coriander Chicken

Ingredients

- 4 chicken breasts, cut into chunks
- 200mls (8fl oz) coconut milk
- 1 teaspoon ground cumin
- 1 teaspoon ground coriander (cilantro)
- 1/2 teaspoon dried oregano
- 1/2 teaspoon chilli powder
- 4 cloves of garlic, finely chopped
- Sea salt
- Freshly ground black pepper

SERVES 4

238 calories per serving

Method

Place all of the ingredients into a slow cooker and stir them well. Cook on low for 6 hours, or until the chicken is cooked through. Serve with brown rice and vegetables.

Sausage Casserole

Ingredients

- 400g (14oz) tin of chopped tomatoes
- 100g (3½ oz) button mushrooms
- 8 good quality sausages
- 2 slices bacon
- 3 carrots, peeled and chopped
- 2 leeks, chopped
- 2 tablespoons cornflour
- 1 swede, peeled and chopped
- 1 tablespoon tomato purée (paste)
- 1 teaspoon paprika
- 1 teaspoon mixed herbs
- 300mls (½ pint) hot beef stock (broth)

SERVES 4

467 calories per serving

Method

Place the sausages under a hot grill (broiler) and brown them for around 4 minutes. Place the sausages, bacon, swede, mushrooms, carrots and leeks into a slow cooker. Add in the tomatoes, purée, paprika, herbs and stock (broth). Cook on low for 8 hours or on high for 4 hours. Mix the cornflour with 2 tablespoons of cold water and mix to a smooth paste. Stir the cornflour mixture into the casserole and allow it to cook for another 15 minutes.

Goulash

Ingredients

- 450g (1lb) stewing steak, cubed
- 400g (14oz) tinned chopped tomatoes
- 2 teaspoons tomato purée (paste)
- 2 cloves of garlic, chopped
- 2 red peppers, (bell peppers), deseeded and chopped
- 1 large onion, peeled and chopped
- 1 tablespoon paprika
- 1 large handful of fresh parsley
- 400mls (14fl oz) beef stock (broth)
- 150mls (5fl oz) crème fraîche
- 1 tablespoon olive oil

SERVES 4

332 calories per serving

Method

Heat the oil in a frying pan, add the steak, garlic and onions and brown them for a few minutes. Transfer it to a slow cooker. Add the remaining ingredients to the slow cooker, except the parsley and creme fraiche and stir well. Cook on low for around 6 hours. Sprinkle in the parsley and stir in the crème fraîche. Serve into bowls.

Cajun Pulled Pork

Ingredients

- 300g (11oz) mushrooms, sliced
- 4 cloves of garlic, chopped
- 2 teaspoons Cajun seasoning
- 1.35kg (3lb) pork shoulder joint
- 1 teaspoon chilli powder
- 1 teaspoon ground coriander (cilantro)
- 1 onion, chopped
- 1 handful of coriander (cilantro) leaves, chopped
- 900mls (1 ½ pints) chicken or vegetable stock (broth)

SERVES 8

371
calories
per serving

Method

Place the Cajun seasoning and chilli powder on a large plate and coat the pork joint in the mixture. Transfer the pork joint to a slow cooker. Add the mushrooms, coriander (cilantro), garlic and onion and pour in the stock (broth). Cook on low for 7-8 hours or until the meat is tender and falling apart. Use 2 forks to pull the meat into shreds before serving.

Beef & Root Vegetables

Ingredients

1.35kg (3lb) beef silverside joint

400g (14oz) tin of chopped tomatoes

3 carrots, peeled and roughly chopped

2 parsnips, peeled and roughly chopped

3 teaspoons dried thyme

2 onions, sliced

1 small swede, peeled and roughly chopped

1 tablespoon cornflour

1 clove garlic, crushed

1 bay leaf

1 handful of fresh parsley, chopped

600mls (1 pint) beef stock (broth)

1 tablespoon vegetable oil

Sea salt

Freshly ground black pepper

SERVES 8

399
calories
per serving

Method

Heat the oil in a large frying pan, add the meat and brown it well on each side. Remove the meat and place it in a slow cooker. Add the onions and garlic to the frying pan and cook them for 4 minutes then add them to the slow cooker. Surround the beef with the tinned tomatoes, vegetables and add in the herbs and stock (broth). Cook on low for 8 hours. Remove the beef from the slow cooker and set it aside, keeping it warm. Combine the cornflour with a tablespoon or two of cold water and mix it until smooth. Stir the cornflour mixture into the slow cooker and let it continue cooking for 10 minutes. Remove the bayleaf. Sprinkle in the parsley and mix well. Slice the beef and serve it along with the vegetables.

Caribbean Citrus Squash

Ingredients

- 3 onions, finely sliced
- 3 cloves of garlic
- 2 butternut squash, peeled and chopped
- 2 teaspoons ground ginger
- 1 red chilli, finely chopped
- 1 small handful of fresh coriander (cilantro), chopped
- 200mls (7fl oz) vegetable stock (broth)
- 2 tablespoons sesame oil
- Juice of 2 large orange
- Juice of 2 limes
- Sea salt
- Freshly ground black pepper

**SERVES
4**

200
calories
per serving

Method

Place all of the ingredients, except the coriander (cilantro) and salt and pepper into a slow cooker and stir them well. Cook on low for 4 hours. Season with salt and pepper. Stir in the fresh coriander (cilantro) just before serving.

Chinese Chicken & Noodles

Ingredients

225g (8oz) egg noodles

4 chicken fillets

2.5cm (1inch) chunk of fresh ginger, peeled and chopped

2 cloves of garlic, chopped

1 onion, peeled and chopped

1 medium sized pak choi (bok choy), coarsely chopped

1 red pepper, (bell pepper), deseeded and sliced

1 small handful of fresh coriander (cilantro) leaves

1 star anise

1/4 teaspoon chili powder

1 teaspoon fish sauce

1 tablespoon tomato purée (paste)

2 tablespoons soy sauce

360mls (12fl oz) hot chicken stock (broth)

**SERVES
4**

306
calories
per serving

Method

Lay the chicken fillets on the bottom of a slow cooker. Add in the garlic, ginger, onion, chilli, star anise, fish sauce, purée (paste), soy sauce and stock (broth) and stir well. Cook on low for around 6 hour. Add the red pepper (bell pepper) and pak choi (bok choy). Cook for a further 20 minutes then sprinkle in the coriander (cilantro) and stir well. In the meantime, cook the noodles according to the instructions. Serve the noodles with the chicken over the top.

Lamb Moussaka

Ingredients

- 450g (1lb) minced (ground) lamb
- 3 cloves of garlic, crushed
- 1 large onion, peeled and chopped
- 1 large aubergine (eggplant) cut into 1cm (1/2 inch) thick slices
- 1 teaspoon ground cinnamon
- 1 tablespoon tomato purée (paste)
- 1 tablespoon plain (all-purpose) flour
- 200mls (7fl oz) lamb or vegetable stock (broth)
- 1 tablespoon olive oil

FOR THE TOPPING:
- 225g (8oz) plain (unflavoured) yoghurt
- 75g (3oz) feta cheese, crumbled
- 3 eggs
- pinch of grated nutmeg

SERVES 4

458 calories per serving

Method

Heat a tablespoon of oil in a frying pan, add the aubergine (eggplant) slices and brown them on each side. Remove them from the pan and set them aside. Add the lamb and onion to the frying pan and brown it for around 5 minutes. Transfer the lamb to a slow cooker. Add the stock (broth), garlic, spices, tomatoes, purée and flour. Cover the lamb mixture with slices of aubergine (eggplant) making sure it completes covers it. Cook on high for 6 hours or on low for 9 hours. In a bowl, mix together the eggs, yogurt, feta cheese and nutmeg. Spread the mixture on top of the aubergine. Continue cooking for around 1 hour until the mixture has set. Place the slow cooker bowl under a hot grill for 2 minutes to brown the topping. Serve with salad or a heap of vegetables.

Tender Five-Spice Beef

Ingredients

450g (1lb) braising steak, cut into strips
5cm (2 inch) chunk of fresh ginger, peeled and grated (shredded)
4 cloves of garlic, finely chopped
2 teaspoons Chinese five-spice powder
2 onions, peeled and thinly sliced
1 tablespoon cornflour
1 teaspoon chilli flakes
360mls (12fl oz) hot beef stock (broth)
4 tablespoon soy sauce
2 tablespoons olive oil
Sea salt
Freshly ground black pepper

SERVES 4

376 calories per serving

Method

Heat the oil in a frying pan, add the onions and cook for 4 minutes. Add the garlic, ginger and chilli and cook for 1 minute. Transfer the onion mixture to a slow cooker. Coat the beef in the five-spice powder then cook it in a hot pan for around 3 minutes to brown it. Place the meat in a slow cooker. Add in the stock (broth) and soy sauce. Cook for 4-5 hours on high. Mix the cornflour with 2 tablespoons of cold water and mix to a smooth paste. Stir the cornflour into the slow cooker. Let it continue cooking for 15 minutes. Season with salt and pepper. Serve with rice and vegetables.

Chicken Cacciatore

Ingredients

750g (1lb 11oz) mushrooms, halved

400g (14oz) tin of chopped tomatoes

4 skinless chicken breasts

3 tablespoons tomato purée (paste)

2 teaspoons dried oregano

3 cloves of garlic, chopped

1 onion, finely chopped

1/4 teaspoon cayenne pepper

200mls (7fl oz) hot chicken stock (broth)

2 tablespoons olive oil

**SERVES
4**

279
calories
per serving

Method

In a bowl, mix together the hot stock (broth) and tomato purée. Place all the other ingredients into a slow cooker and pour the hot stock (broth) on top. Cook on low for around 6 hours. Serve with brown rice or quinoa and vegetables.

Pulled Chicken & Lettuce Wraps

Ingredients

4 skinless chicken breasts

4 large tomatoes, roughly chopped

4 medium sized onions, peeled and chopped

4 cloves of garlic, chopped

2 teaspoon ground ginger

1/2 teaspoon ground cinnamon

2 teaspoons fresh basil, chopped

1 teaspoon chilli powder

1 teaspoon cloves

1 iceberg or romaine lettuce, leaves separated

100mls (3½ fl oz) hot water

SERVES 4

244 calories per serving

Method

Place all of the ingredients, except the lettuce, into a slow cooker and stir well. Cook on low for around 6 hours. Use a fork to pull the chicken into shreds and mix it thoroughly with the other ingredients. To serve, spoon the pulled chicken mixture into lettuce leaves and fold them over. Alternatively, transfer it to a serving dish for everyone to help themselves.

Pork, Mustard & Apple Casserole

Ingredients

6 boneless pork chops

3 apples, peeled, cored and sliced

2 onions, peeled and sliced

1 small handful of fresh sage leaves, chopped

450mls (15fl oz) hot chicken or vegetable stock (broth)

2 teaspoons wholegrain mustard

SERVES 6

196 calories per serving

Method

Lay the pork chops on the bottom of the slow cooker. Scatter the sage leaves over the top and add a layer of apples and onions. Add the mustard to the hot stock (broth) and mix well. Pour the stock (broth) into the slow cooker. Cook on low for 7 hours or until the chops are completely cooked. Serve with a heap of vegetables or mash.

Pork Curry

Ingredients

450g (1lb) pork steaks, cut into chunks

2 red peppers, (bell peppers) deseeded and chopped

2 cloves of garlic, crushed

2 teaspoons ground ginger

1 stalk of lemongrass (inner leaves only)

1 large onion, peeled and chopped

1 red chilli pepper, deseeded and chopped

1 teaspoon ground cumin

1 teaspoon ground coriander

1 teaspoon paprika

1/2 teaspoon salt

1/2 teaspoon pepper

Juice of 1 lime

360mls (12fl oz) coconut milk

1 tablespoon olive oil

SERVES 4

415 calories per serving

Method

Heat the oil in a frying pan, add the pork and brown it for a few minutes. Transfer the pork to a slow cooker. Add all of the other ingredients, except the peppers, to the pot and stir really well. Cook for 6 hours or until the pork becomes tender. Add the peppers and cook for another 30 minutes. Remove the lemongrass before serving. Can be served with brown rice or cauliflower rice as a low carb alternative.

Chicken & Ham Pie

Ingredients

100g (3½ oz) thick cut ham, diced

100g (3½ oz) crème fraîche, optional

25g (1oz) butter

4 large chicken breasts, cut into chunks

2 leeks, chopped

2 tablespoons plain flour (all-purpose flour)

1 sheet of readymade puff pastry

1 onion, peeled and chopped

1 teaspoon dried thyme

1 teaspoon dried parsley

360mls (12fl oz) chicken stock (broth)

1 teaspoon olive oil

SERVES 4

552 calories per serving

Method

Heat the olive oil in a pan, add the chicken and onions and brown them for 5 minutes. Transfer the chicken to a slow cooker. Add the leeks and herbs to the mixture. Place the butter in the frying pan and allow it to melt. Remove it from the heat and whisk in the flour until it is smooth and creamy. Gradually add the stock (broth) to the butter mixture and whisk until smooth. Pour the stock (broth) into the slow cooker. Cook on low for 4-5 hours or until the chicken is tender. Allow the mixture to cool slightly. When ready to assemble the pie, stir the crème fraîche and ham into the chicken mixture. Transfer the chicken and ham filling to a pie dish. Roll out the pastry and cover the top of the dish, trimming around the edges. Preheat the oven to 180C/360F and cook the pie for 35-40 minutes or until the pastry is golden.

Slow Cooked Meat Loaf

Ingredients

675g (1 ½lb) minced (ground) beef

100g (3 ½ oz) mushrooms, finely chopped

2 slices of brown bread, crumbed

2 eggs, beaten

1 teaspoon onion powder

1 teaspoon dried parsley

½ teaspoon salt

½ teaspoon dried sage

120mls (4fl oz) milk

1 teaspoon Worcestershire sauce

**SERVES
6**

247
calories
per serving

Method

In a large bowl, combine the eggs, onion powder, breadcrumbs, salt, mushrooms, sage, parsley, milk and Worcestershire sauce. Add in the minced (ground) beef and mix it well. Using clean hands form the mixture into a round. Place it in the slow cooker and cook on low for 6 hours. Allow it to rest for 10 minutes before slicing and serving.

Salmon & Cannellini Mash

Ingredients

4 salmon fillets

2 x 400g (14oz) tins of cooked cannellini beans

2 tablespoons crème fraîche

1 onion, peeled and chopped

360mls (12fl oz) hot fish or vegetable stock (broth)

1 teaspoon mustard

Zest and juice of 1 lemon

1 small bunch of parsley

Sea salt

Freshly ground black pepper

SERVES 4

459 calories per serving

Method

Place the beans, onion, mustard, lemon and stock (broth) into a slow cooker and stir well. Season with salt and pepper. Lay the fish fillets on top of the beans. Cook on low for 2 hours or until the fish is completely cooked and is beginning to flake. Lift out the fish and set it aside. Drain off the liquid from the cooker, leaving the bean mixture in the cooker. Mash the cannellini beans together with the crème fraîche and stir in the parsley. Serve with the fish on top of the mash.

Chicken Wings

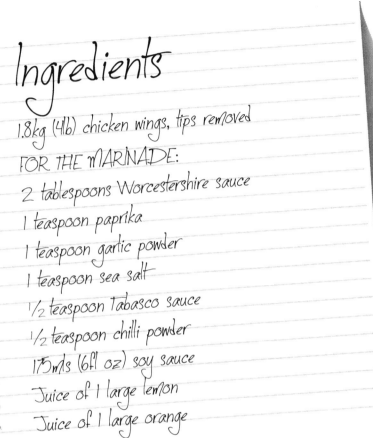

Ingredients

1.8kg (4lb) chicken wings, tips removed

FOR THE MARINADE:

2 tablespoons Worcestershire sauce

1 teaspoon paprika

1 teaspoon garlic powder

1 teaspoon sea salt

1/2 teaspoon Tabasco sauce

1/2 teaspoon chilli powder

175mls (6fl oz) soy sauce

Juice of 1 large lemon

Juice of 1 large orange

**SERVES
6**

492
calories
per serving

Method

Place all of the ingredients for the marinade into a bowl and mix well. Add the chicken wings and coat them in the mixture. Allow them to marinade for at least half an hour and longer if you can. Transfer the chicken wings to a slow cooker. Cook on low for 5 hours. Serve into a platter for sharing. Enjoy.

Desserts & Puddings

Chocolate Brownies

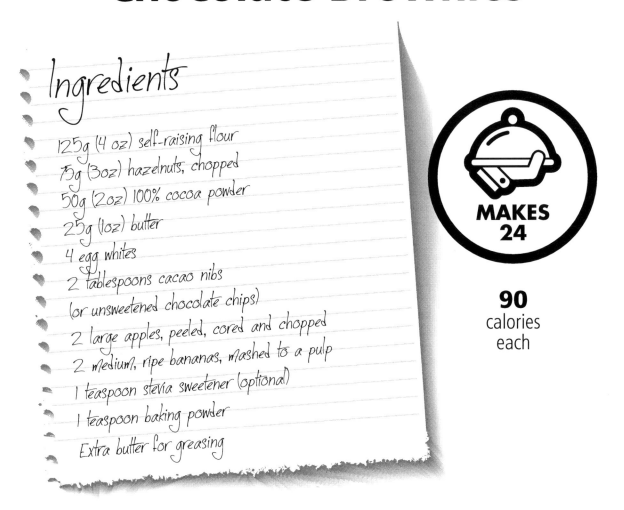

Ingredients

- 125g (4 oz) self-raising flour
- 75g (3oz) hazelnuts, chopped
- 50g (2oz) 100% cocoa powder
- 25g (1oz) butter
- 4 egg whites
- 2 tablespoons cacao nibs (or unsweetened chocolate chips)
- 2 large apples, peeled, cored and chopped
- 2 medium, ripe bananas, mashed to a pulp
- 1 teaspoon stevia sweetener (optional)
- 1 teaspoon baking powder
- Extra butter for greasing

MAKES 24

90 calories each

Method

First, you need to line the slow cooker with greaseproof paper. Cut out an oval shaped piece of greaseproof paper by drawing around the bottom of the bowl. Insert the paper and coat it and the sides of the cooker with butter. Place the chopped apples into a saucepan with just enough hot water to cover the bottom of the pan and gently warm them for 10 minutes until the apple has softened then mash until smooth then set it aside. Place the cocoa powder, baking powder, hazelnuts, cacao nibs (chocolate chips, flour and stir. In another bowl, mix together the butter, bananas, eggs, apples, stevia (if using) and mix well. Mix the wet ingredients into the dry and combine them thoroughly. Transfer the mixture to the slow cooker. Cook on low for 4 hours. Use a palette knife cut the mixture from the sides of the slow cooker them tip it out. Allow it to cool before slicing and serving.

Lemon & Coconut Rice Pudding

Ingredients

- 100g (3 1/2 oz) short grain brown rice
- 2 tablespoons toasted coconut chips (unsweetened)
- 1-2 teaspoons stevia sweetener
- 1 teaspoon vanilla extract
- 1 teaspoon grated (shredded) lemon zest
- 1/2 teaspoon salt
- 600mls (1 pint) coconut water
- 400mls (14fl oz) coconut milk
- Butter for greasing

MAKES 4

299 calories per serving

Method

Coat the inside of a slow cooker with butter. Add the rice, coconut water, coconut milk, stevia, vanilla and salt and mix the ingredients well. Cook on low for 4-5 hours. Sprinkle in the lemon zest and stir. Allow the lemon to infuse for a few minutes. Serve into bowls and garnish with toasted coconut chips. You can all serve with fresh fruit, hot or cold.

Chocolate Rice Pudding

Ingredients

- 100g (3 1/2 oz) short grain brown rice
- 2-3 teaspoons stevia sweetener
- 1 1/2 tablespoons 100% cocoa powder
- 1/2 teaspoon ground cinnamon
- 1/2 teaspoon ground nutmeg
- 1 teaspoon vanilla extract
- 750mls (1 1/2 pints) milk
- 150mls (5fl oz) double cream (heavy cream)

SERVES 4

396
calories
per serving

Method

Place the rice, milk, cocoa powder, cream and stevia into a slow cooker and stir well. Sprinkle in the cinnamon, nutmeg and vanilla extract and mix together. Cook on low for 4-5 hours or until the rice is soft and creamy. Serve on its own or add some fruit such as chopped fresh apricots or a handful of berries.

Banana Bread

Ingredients

200g (7oz) plain flour (all-purpose flour)
120g (4oz) butter
4 large ripe bananas, mashed to a pulp
3 teaspoons stevia sweetener (optional)
2 eggs
1 teaspoon baking powder
1/2 teaspoon baking soda
1/2 teaspoon salt
1/4 teaspoon ground cinnamon
Butter for greasing

SERVES 6

271 calories per serving

Method

In a bowl, combine the eggs, butter and stevia (if using). Stir in the bananas, flour, cinnamon, baking soda, baking powder and salt and mix really well. Grease a loaf tin which sits easily inside your slow cooker. Spoon the bread mixture into the tin. Cook on low for 4 hours. Allow it to cool then slice and serve.

Stuffed Apples

Ingredients

4 large apples, core removed
2 teaspoons stevia sweetener
100g (3½ oz) walnuts, finely chopped
50g (2oz) oats
25g (1oz) butter, cut into flakes
½ teaspoon ground cinnamon

SERVES 4

345
calories
per serving

Method

In a bowl, combine the oats, butter, stevia, cinnamon and walnuts. Mix until well combined. Spoon some of the mixture into the hole where the core was removed from the apples. Place the apples upright in a slow cooker and add just enough water to cover the bottom of the slow cooker. Cook on low for 3 hours. Serve with yogurt, cream or crème fraîche. Enjoy.

Poached Peaches

Ingredients

100g (3 ½ oz) fresh blueberries

4 large peaches (or 6 small), halved and stone removed

1 teaspoon ground ginger

75mls (3 fl oz) freshly squeezed orange juice

**SERVES
4**

68
calories
per serving

Method

Lay the peach halves, flat side down, on the bottom of a slow cooker. Sprinkle on the ginger, pour in the orange juice and add the blueberries. Cook on low for 90 minutes. Serve on their own or with a dollop of plain yogurt or crème fraîche.

Fruit Compote

Ingredients

900g (2lb) frozen mixed berries
1½ tablespoons cornflour
75mls (3 fl oz) freshly squeezed orange juice
1-2 teaspoons stevia sweetener (optional)
2 tablespoons water

SERVES 6

54
calories
per serving

Method

Place the berries, orange juice and stevia into a slow cooker and stir well Cook on high for 90 minutes. Mix together the cornflour and water and stir until it becomes smooth. Pour the mixture into the berries. Allow it to cook for 15 minutes, stirring occasionally. Serve with a dollop of Greek yogurt or crème fraîche.

Fresh Custard & Raspberries

Ingredients

- 200g (7oz) raspberries
- 4 large eggs, preferably free-range
- 2-3 teaspoons of stevia sweetener, or to taste
- 1 teaspoon cornflour
- 1 teaspoon vanilla extract
- 450mls (15fl oz) full-fat milk
- Hot water

SERVES 4

164
calories
per serving

Method

Mix the cornflour with a tablespoon of the milk until it becomes smooth. Gently whisk the eggs and stir in the cornflour mixture, milk, stevia and vanilla extract. Use a heatproof dish which fits inside your slow cooker and pour the egg mixture into it. Cover the dish with silver foil and place it in the centre of the slow cooker. Pour hot water into the slow cooker until it comes around half way up the dish inside it. Cook on high for around 3 hours. Remove the custard from the cooker and pour it into bowls. Allow it to cool slightly then sprinkle on the raspberries. Serve and eat immediately.

You may also be interested in other titles by
Erin Rose Publishing
which are available in both paperback and ebook.

 Quick Start Guides

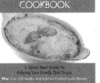

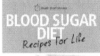

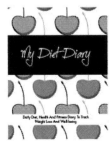
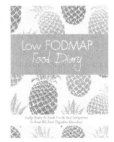

Books by Sophie Ryan
Erin Rose Publishing

30 Simple And Delicious Superfood Energy Balls And Bites
Recipes For Great Health and Wellbeing

Over 30 Easy And Delicious Superfood Energy Bars
Recipes To Boost Your Vitality

30 Simple And Tasty Energy Shots And Smoothies
To Power Up Your Health And Well-Being

Printed in Great Britain
by Amazon